A Journey

Through Time

Time

London Transport Photographs 1880 to 1965

Sheila Taylor

With picture research by
Hugh Robertson and
Simon Murphy

Laurence King

Published 1992 by Laurence King

A catalogue record for this book is
available from the British Library
ISBN 1 85669 022 9

Designed by Michael Phillips/Archetype
Printed in Singapore by Imago

The author would like to thank Oliver Green,
former Curator of the London Transport
Museum, for reading the text and making
helpful editorial suggestions. Thanks also to Paul
Castle of the London Transport Museum for his
encouragement and enthusiasm during the
preparation of this book, and Janette Palmer for
typing the manuscript and captions. I am most
grateful to Bryce Beaumont, who worked in the
London Transport Publicity Office in the 1930s,
and to Michael Robbins, former London
Transport Managing Director (Railways) for
their help and advice concerning the history of
the photographic collection; thanks also to Dr
Heinz Zinram for his personal reminiscences.
Special thanks to Bryan Bronson and Sue
Broadbent for printing the photographs for this
book to such a high professional standard. I am
particularly grateful to Colin Tait who, over the
last four decades, has taken so many excellent
photographs for London Transport. Finally I
would like to thank Jane Havell and Joanne
Lightfoot of Calmann & King Ltd; Jane for
initiating the project and Joanne for being such a
patient editor.

Title page:
A view from the driver's cab of the two
Bakerloo Line platforms at Piccadilly
Circus station, looking south.

Heinz Zinram
22 June 1954

Photograph numbers 160

Public transport in London before 1800 was provided by watermen plying their wherries on the River Thames, then London's main traffic artery. Wheeled transport was slow to develop, as the narrow and rutted roads made it easier to walk than ride. It was not until 1829 that London's first bus service opened, linking Paddington and the Bank. The first bus was the horse-drawn omnibus, originally developed in France. This soon became popular and by the 1840s had completely replaced the existing hackney hire coaches in London.

In these early years many bus companies sprang up and there was fierce competition between them. After several take-over bids, the London General Omnibus Company (LGOC) emerged as the dominant operator; by the 1890s it was carrying well over one hundred million passengers a year. The motor bus had become a viable alternative to horse power by the beginning of the twentieth century, and once again the LGOC took the lead, absorbing its main rivals.

Transport Through a Lens

Motive power also revolutionized the tramways, which had been horse-powered since 1861 when trams were first introduced to London from America. The first electric tram service, operated by the London United Tramways, opened in 1901 to serve the western suburbs of London. Tram companies mushroomed over the next few years, the London County Council operating the most extensive system. Trams were to remain an important form of transport in the city until 1952.

The story of London's underground trains begins in 1863, when the first urban underground railway in the world, the Metropolitan Railway, opened between Paddington and Farringdon. The trains were hauled by steam locomotives. Despite the dire warnings of inherent dangers by the press, the Metropolitan was an immediate success and the line was quickly extended in both directions. In 1868 a second company, the Metropolitan District Railway (District), opened a line from South Kensington to Westminster; this line was also soon extended. Eventually, the Metropolitan and District Railways joined up at both ends to form the Inner Circle underground railway in 1884. Both companies expanded their respective services, constructing overground extensions into the London suburbs.

The Metropolitan and District Railways used the cut and cover construction method, but this caused severe disruption at street level. The problem could be avoided by tunnelling under London. Following the successful construction of two tunnels under the Thames in 1843 and 1870, the first electric deep tube railway, the City and South London (C&SLR), was opened in 1890. Six more deep level tube lines opened at the turn of the century, each built by a separate company: Waterloo and City (1898), Central London (1900), Great Northern and City (1904), Bakerloo (1906), Piccadilly (1906) and Hampstead Tube (1907). The existing Metropolitan and District Railways were mostly electrified during the same period.

The Creation of London Transport

All these road and underground developments were expensive, and a number of companies failed or were merged with larger, more financially secure concerns. In 1902 the Underground Electric Railways of London Co. Ltd (UERL) was founded. It expanded rapidly and came to dominate London's public transport operations. Over a period of eleven years the UERL took control of the District Railway, five tube companies, the private electric tram companies and the giant bus operator, the LGOC. (The Metropolitan Railway, the various council tramways and suburban rail services remained independent.) With all these subsidiaries under its wing, the UERL became known as the Underground Group, sometimes referred to as the London Traffic Combine.

The dominance of the Combine did not deter competition from smaller concerns, however, particularly the independent bus companies. In 1933 the Government, believing that this unrestricted competition was not in the public interest, created a single authority, the London Passenger Transport Board (LPTB), to be responsible for all London's public transport. The LPTB took over

A view from the Bank of England, showing the Mansion House, Cheapside and Queen Victoria Street. As can be seen by the volume of traffic, the horse-drawn omnibus was the main form of transport in the City at the time.

c. 1902

the Underground Group's road and rail operations, the council tramways, the Metropolitan Railway and all the independent bus companies. It soon became known as London Transport.

The beginning of construction work on new escalators at Trafalgar Square Underground station (renamed Charing Cross in 1979).

Topical Press
April 1925

Historical Photographs

London Transport, and the various companies which preceded it, sought to document every aspect of the development of London's public transport services through photography, and in doing so created an invaluable historic record. The purpose of this book is not to give a history of London Transport, but to explore the riches to be found in its black and white photographic collection. The photographs featured, many of which are being published for the first time, have been chosen for their intrinsic value as works of art, their interesting subject matter, or simply because they are striking images. The material has great breadth and variety. Many photographs illustrate London Transport's concern for design. In every aspect of its operations – from stations, bus garages and vehicles, to such details as lighting, lettering and ticket machines – it aimed for the highest standards of design. During the 1920s and 1930s, the design policies of the Vice Chairman, Frank Pick, stamped the company with a corporate identity which was to become internationally recognized.

Some photographs depict people working behind the scenes, often at night, to keep the transport system moving. There are staff doing jobs of which the public is largely unaware: catching rats or cleaning the railway tracks by hand. Not forgotten are the construction workers who sweated in the dark bowels of the earth to tunnel their way under London. Other photographs show staff relaxing over cups of tea during a shift break, or enjoying leisure and sporting activities laid on by the company.

The photographs taken during both World Wars illustrate the diversity of London Transport's war effort. Staff were involved on both fronts, literally and figuratively, with vehicles sent to the war zone, and staff at home on the lookout for enemy aircraft.

As well as its staff, London Transport recorded the people using its services, travelling on the trains and buses, or simply making an enquiry at a lost property counter. Photographs depicting Londoners waiting for trams have now become documents of social history. Many of the older photographs of the streets of London, too, provide a wealth of historical information, whether it be of architectural, geographical or social interest. Some of the photographs in the collection will never be more than the visual record they were intended to be, but often a routine shot has been turned into a work of art through the photographer's skill with lighting and camera angle, and eye for the potential human story behind the image.

Recording the Early Years

London Transport's collection of photographs has been in the Museum's care since 1986. The nucleus of the collection was formed from photographs taken by the photographic agency Topical Press Ltd which, since about 1906, had been commissioned by the Underground Electric Railway Company of London to take photographs for company records. These focused on the work of the Underground, including construction, new stations, signalling developments and various engineering projects. Topical Press held the negatives, while prints were kept by the Underground.

When the London Passenger Transport Board was created, it continued to commission photographs recording every aspect of its operations in minute detail for both technical and publicity purposes. Many photographs were taken specifically to illustrate the staff magazine. Originally titled *T.O.T. Staff Magazine* (after the "Train Omnibus Tram" employees' mutual aid fund), this was launched in October 1922 and appeared monthly. Following the creation of London Transport, the magazine was re-launched with a new name, *Pennyfare*. There was a further name change in 1947 when *London Transport Magazine* became available to the public through newsagents at a cost of two pence. The magazine, which was produced every month until March 1973, was packed with commissioned photographs.

Photographs were taken throughout the Second World War, mostly recording London Transport's invaluable contribution to the war effort and the devastating effects of bombing. After the war, the photographic collection became the responsibility of the Publicity Office, and it was decided

that the scope of the collection should be enlarged. The fine work done in the 1930s by photo-journalists, such as Bert Hardy and Bill Brandt, encouraged the Office to commission some of the innovative and talented photographers then working in Britain. One of these was Dr Heinz Zinram, an Austrian photographer who undertook many commissions for London Transport from 1947 up until the early 1970s. A lawyer by training, he was interned in England during the war and sent to Australia. After the war, he made his way back to London and set up as a photographer. One of his specializations was portrait photography; he took pictures of most of London Transport's officers and officials. (It was customary in London Transport at that time to photograph staff whenever they were promoted.) As well as working in black and white, Zinram was a talented colour photographer, and in the 1960s devised new techniques for developing colour. He worked for *Time-Life* and several national museums as well as London Transport. He now lives in retirement in Oxfordshire.

Another skilful photographer was Colin Tait. His talents were utilized by London Transport as soon as his "demob" papers came through in 1947. His work covered most aspects of London Transport's activities. Much of it involved shooting at night or in the early hours of the morning, and yet its quality suggests no hurry or impatience but a determination to get the photograph right, often in awkward conditions of light and space. Tait has continued to accept commissions from London Transport and still prints

A shunter operating a points lever at Northfields Depot, which was a main stabling point for trains when not in service.

Colin Tait
March 1955

photographs for the Museum, often from his own original negatives which were produced more than 40 years ago.

Several other photographers worked on a commission basis for London Transport, though not quite so extensively as Zinram and Tait. Some, though not all, are represented in this book, and include Walter A. Curtin, W.H.R. Godwin, J. Somerset Murray, Dell and Wainwright, H.J. Hare, Sidney Newbery, H.K. Nolan and Paul Proctor.

A Photographic Treasure-Trove

In the early 1950s there was a crisis within the Publicity Office when it was announced that Topical Press was about to be made bankrupt. This meant that the negatives of photographs commissioned by London Transport and its predecessors would no longer be accessible. Among these negatives were photographs taken in the 1920s and 1930s, when many great designers and artists were making their name through their work for London Transport. A swift decision was made to buy the negatives and thus secure the unique photographic records for posterity.

Southgate station is an outstanding example of the work of Charles Holden and is now a listed building. While epitomizing Holden's distinctive 1930s design style, Southgate has a unique layout. The corner site was developed to include the station at the centre, with a bus station, shops and waiting room behind it and a grassed traffic island in the foreground.

Topical Press
April 1935

This Topical Press collection consists of over 65,000 glass plate negatives. Although several independent photographers kept their negatives, which are no longer traceable, W.H.R. Godwin and Colin Tait donated theirs to the London Transport Museum. The total number of black and white images in the Museum's care is now well over 100,000.

As well as the photographs specifically commissioned by London Transport, there are others in the collection which have come from unexpected sources. Many albums of a specialist nature have been donated by private collectors, and there are a large number of photographs which have been brought together over the years by enthusiastic members of staff with a sense of history and an interest in photography.

The best of these are eleven albums of photographs of London, put together by Charles White, a writer and resident historian in the Publicity Office in the 1930s. The photographs date mainly from the 1920s, but some go back as far as 1896. White was responsible for writing the *Country Walks*, a series of booklets designed to encourage people to travel to the countryside by Underground, bus or Green Line coach. The photograph albums were

A quiet moment in St James's Park, away from the bustle of the city. Photographs like this one were taken to encourage people to visit London's varied attractions – and to use public transport to get there.

Topical Press
7 February 1939

something he took upon himself, in addition to his full-time writing work. The captions he wrote for the photographs in his albums often contain detailed descriptions, giving considerable historical, sociological and architectural information. Laced with White's personal views and somewhat idiosyncratic comments, they make interesting and amusing reading today.

The Publicity Office also collected several albums of scenic views, taken both in London and the surrounding countryside, many of which were used to illustrate the *Country Walks*. These provide a contrast to the record photographs which depict the latest engineering developments or new building work, in that they were taken to achieve a certain mood, and their subject matter has a more subtle link to London Transport.

As well as writing *Country Walks*, Charles White helped to put together the text which accompanied London Transport's lantern lectures. These were an important tool in the Publicity Office's campaign to promote London Transport and were provided free of charge. They consisted of seven ready-to-read lectures on London and London's traffic, and were illustrated by a set of glass lantern slides, packed in special wooden boxes and despatched by passenger train throughout London and the surrounding counties. Many of the slides were copied from photographs taken by Topical Press. Lantern slides later gave way to film-strip projectors, and both were eventually superseded by television. Both the film strips and slides, still in their original boxes, are now part of the Museum's photographic collection.

The Collection Today

Since the 1950s, London Transport's photographic collection has been moved on more than one occasion. In 1984 it became the responsibility of the Advertising and Publicity Department at 55 Broadway. Unfortunately, storage space was then at a premium and the heavy glass plate negatives could no longer be housed at London Transport headquarters but were held off-site, making access problematic. The photographic albums were copied on to microfiche for viewing by members of the public.

When the London Transport Museum took over responsibility for the care and management of the photographic collection, including both black and white, and colour photographs, in 1986, a special store was constructed at premises in North London so that black and white negatives could be housed in a suitably controlled environment. A small team has been cataloguing the collection ever since, using a specially written computer program. This provides more efficient and faster access to information about the photographs. Today, the Museum continues to commission new photography in order to document all aspects of London Transport and its subsidiaries, and to provide a historical record for future generations.

Horse Power to Motor Transport

Transport in London, which had been dominated by the horse for most of the nineteenth century, was to change rapidly with the development of electric traction and the internal combustion engine. In 1890 the world's first electric tube railway, the City and South London (C&SLR), was opened. This ran between King William Street in the City and Stockwell on the other side of the River Thames. By 1907, all the London Underground rail services had been electrified, apart from the Metropolitan steam service north of Harrow.

A similar rate of progress occurred above ground. The London General Omnibus Company (LGOC) had been formed in 1856 and had quickly become the largest single bus company operating horse buses in London. The first decade of the twentieth century saw the motor bus gradually replace the horse-drawn omnibus, and in 1910 the LGOC started manufacturing its own standard motor bus, the B-Type.

Horse-drawn tram services began to be replaced in 1901 when, after unsuccessful experiments with steam and cable haulage, London United Tramways opened London's first electrified route. Other companies quickly followed suit, and by 1915 the horse tram had disappeared from London's streets.

The reliability, speed and comfort of these new forms of public transport encouraged people to use them. Travel was no longer the prerogative of the middle and upper classes as working-class people could afford the lower fares. Bus companies advertised day trips to the country, and one Underground company laid on special trains to the seaside at weekends.

The photographs in this chapter reflect the changes from horse power to motorized transport and from steam to electric trains. They also show the development of the infrastructure required to support these changes: the construction of stations and tram routes, the provision of amenities for the staff who operated the services, and the publicity produced to persuade the public to use them. The photographs come from a variety of sources. Many were drawn from the various companies in operation before the establishment of the London Passenger Transport Board in 1933, some having been commissioned for company records. Others were collected by interested individuals such as Charles White, who appreciated their historical significance. Unfortunately, few of the photographers' names were recorded.

Finchley Road station opened in 1879 as part of the Metropolitan Railway. This photograph illustrates the Underground's early use of posters to attract passengers. Even its horse-drawn goods vehicle is functioning as a billboard. Wood Lane station was situated within the White City Exhibition Grounds where the Japan–British Exhibition was running at the time of this photograph. The distinctive illuminated Underground sign became the symbol for all the underground railways in London in 1908.

1910

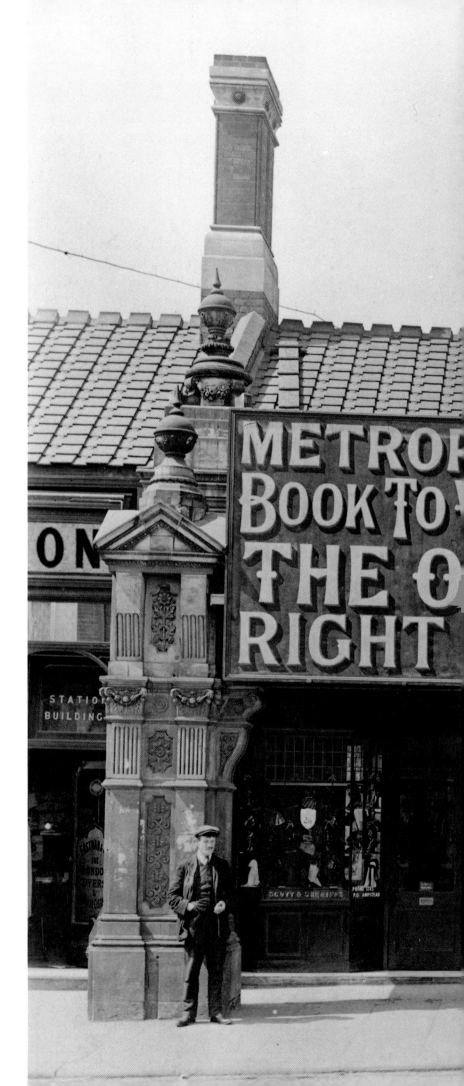

Open-top motor buses in Cheapside.
The church of St Mary-le-Bow,
which houses the famous Bow Bells,
provides a backdrop. Buses still run
along this same number 8 route to
Old Ford. Route numbers were
first introduced on the "Vanguard"
fleet in 1906 and became standard
throughout the London General
Omnibus Company in 1908.

F.H.S. Radlett
1909

A horse bus on the south side of
Trafalgar Square with the National
Gallery in the background. The
word "Atlas" on the side of the bus
indicates the route worked by an
association of proprietors. "Atlas"
was one of the few route
associations to survive the century,
alongside "Times", "Favourite",
"Paragon" and "Royal Blue". The
"Atlas" route ran from the Eyre
Arms in St John's Wood to the
Red Lion at Camberwell Gate.
This seven mile journey took just
over one hour.

c. 1890

This photograph, taken at Aldgate tram
terminus, shows that traffic
congestion is not a modern
phenomenon. Buses and trams
jostle with steam-driven goods
vehicles and hand-drawn carts,
while a single policeman looks
on helplessly.

1914

A platform view of Aldersgate Street (now Barbican) station, taken at midnight to illustrate the newly installed electric lighting by the Electric Generator and Light Company. The original gas lights are still in position, suspended from the roof.

Henry Dixon
22 April 1880

An unusual view, taken from Temple Gardens, of Temple station, which was part of the District Railway. The hansom cabs in the foreground were the taxis of the day. Some old Thames barges are just visible in the background.

1899

BELOW: Passengers on the platform at High Street Kensington station in the days when first- and third-class tickets were issued. In 1883 a first-class single fare from High Street Kensington to Charing Cross cost 9*d* while the third-class fare was 5*d*. First-class accommodation was withdrawn from London Transport trains in 1940 as part of the war economy, with the exception of trains to Aylesbury and Watford, where first-class fares continued to be sold until October 1941.

1892

Emergency work at Farringdon following flooding. Two horse-drawn fire engines mounted in railway wagons are pumping out the water, with a further pump attached to a steam locomotive on the right.

6 May 1915

A London Tramways Company horse tram on the route between Tooting and Blackfriars Bridge.

c. 1890

A group photograph of the staff of the
City and South London Railway at
Stockwell Depot in front of one of
London's first electric tube trains.

c. 1893

London County Council trams on
Westminster Bridge Road. The
single-deck car was specially
designed for use through the
subway between Holborn and the
Embankment.

21 June 1912

A Straker-Squire motor bus belonging to the Great Eastern London Motor Omnibus Company, one of the many bus proprietors operating in London. The Straker-Squire fleet of the Great Eastern was the first to be provided with interior electric lighting; illumination had previously been supplied by oil or acetylene lamps. The Great Eastern was absorbed by the London General Omnibus Company in 1911.

c. 1910

A London General Omnibus driver is checked by the "Timekeeper", the precursor of today's inspector. He is driving a B-Type bus, one of London's earliest reliable motor buses and the first in the world to be mass-produced.

May 1911

The staff canteen at Cricklewood Bus
    Garage.

    c. 1912

The Mayor of Kingston upon Thames,
    Alderman H.C. Minnitt, has just
    wielded the first pick-axe as a signal
    for 400 men to begin digging up
    Kingston Road, Malden. This was
    part of a ceremony to mark the
    start of construction work by the
    London United Tramways.

    3 April 1905

The interior of a booking office at
Golders Green station, northern
terminus of the Charing Cross,
Euston and Hampstead Railway.

1912

The Mayor of Kingston upon Thames
about to drive the first tram across
Kingston Bridge. Clifton Robinson,
the Managing Director of London
United Tramways, stands on the
right of the tram. Robinson had the
use of his own personal tramcar; his
driver, Lewis Bruce, stands on the
platform next to the Mayor.

1 March 1906

These three photographs were taken at Southend-on-Sea shortly before the First World War when day trips out of London were becoming more affordable. Excursions were encouraged by the railway companies, with offers of cheap fares on some services. Passengers could travel on the electrified District Railway as far as East Ham or Barking, beyond which trains were hauled by the steam locomotives of the London Tilbury and Southend Railway (taken over by the Midland Railway in 1912). The joint slogan of the two companies was "Southend and Westcliff-on-Sea for Sea Breezes".

1910–1914

Supporting the War Effort

1914 to 1918

One of the initial effects of the First World War on London's transport was a shortage of vehicles as over 1,300 motor buses and drivers were commandeered for the war effort, both at home and abroad. More than 300 drivers from the London General Omnibus Company volunteered to take their B-Type buses from the streets of London to northern France and Belgium. There, they ferried British troops to the front line, returning with battle-weary soldiers and sometimes the wounded. The sturdy B-Types also proved invaluable over the next four years as supply carriers, ambulances, wireless equipment centres and mobile lofts for carrier pigeons. Many were stripped down to their chassis and converted into lorries, field kitchens, armoured cars and mobile anti-aircraft gun carriages. During their wartime service the B-Types became known affectionately as "Ole Bill" after the cartoonist Bruce Bairnsfather's caricature.

At home, increased passenger traffic, caused by troop movements and the influx of workers for the developing war industries, meant that London's transport system was severely stretched. Also, the Associated Equipment Company (AEC), the bus manufacturing arm of the LGOC, turned to the production of military vehicles, with the result that the buses pressed into war service could not easily be replaced. For Londoners this meant a reduction in services and overcrowding on the buses which did run.

The mobilization of men at the front also had an effect on the work-force at home. Faced with a need to find replacements for the men who had joined up, the transport companies began to employ women to do traditionally male jobs. This was done with great reluctance on the part of both the trade unions and male management. In March 1915 a temporary policy of "women substitutes" was agreed by the Underground. However, when Maida Vale station on the new Bakerloo Line extension was opened in June, it was staffed entirely by women, and in November London's first women bus conductor started work. As well as working in the service areas as conductors, ticket collectors, porters, lift attendants and guards, women were employed in maintenance sections as painters, mechanics and vehicle cleaners. As soon as the war was over, they had to give up their jobs to men returning from active service.

Some of the photographs featured in this chapter were commissioned by the transport companies; others were taken by photo-journalists and correspondents sent out to cover the war. Once again, in many cases, the name of the photographer was not recorded.

Women cleaning a bus at the London
    General Omnibus Company's
    Willesden garage.

1916–1918

Women were employed by the
    Underground during the war from
    1915. This woman is working as a
    station painter.

1915–1918

Women overhaul a bus chassis in a
London General Omnibus
Company engineering shop. The
LGOC employed women from
1916, and by the end of the war
had taken on more than 3,500.

1916–1918

Bus conductors trying their new uniforms for size. Nearly half the women who joined the London General Omnibus Company as conductors gave their previous occupation as "domestic servant".

c. 1915

A ticket collector checks a passenger's ticket at an Underground station.

c. 1915

A female lift attendant prepares to close the lift doors at an Underground station. A uniformed soldier in the background provides a reminder that the country is at war.

c. 1915

A female guard signalling the impending departure of a Metropolitan Railway train bound for Neasden. The Metropolitan Railway was employing 522 women in a wide variety of jobs by the end of 1917.

May 1917

The need to send buses to the front during the First World War caused a shortage at home. One temporary solution was the use of lorries, lent to the London General Omnibus Company by the War Department. In this photograph a conductor stands on the staircase attached to the back of the lorry. A tarpaulin cover could be erected over the frame in bad weather. Lorry-buses were in use from 2 June 1919 to 13 January 1920.

Topical Press
1919

London General Omnibus Company B-Type buses were heavily used during the First World War, at home and on the Western Front. Here soldiers attend to the engine of a B-Type bus which has been converted into a lorry for use by the British army.

Alfieri
1914–1918

An army recruiting sergeant distributing
leaflets on the top of a London bus.

1914–1918

This B-Type bus has been placed at the disposal of the army and converted into a loft for carrier pigeons.

Topical Press
1914–1918

British soldiers with a pipe-smoking French comrade. The buses in the background are camouflaged London General Omnibus Company B-Types, taken to the Western Front and used to ferry troops to the battle areas.

Underwood & Underwood
1914–1918

Locals surround British armoured cars
and B-Type buses, still bearing their
advertising slogans, on war service
in Belgium.

1914–1918

1918 to 1924

Construction in the Twenties

Although the First World War had disrupted many of the plans for developing London's transport systems, the 1920s were years of renewal and activity on several fronts. The Underground secured financial guarantees from the Government to enable it to begin the New Works Programme agreed before the war. By 1923 the complete reconstruction of the City and South London Railway had begun. The aim was to make the dimensions of its tunnels consistent with those of the other railways. Work was also under way on a complex junction linking up the C&SLR with the Hampstead Tube at Camden Town, and on the construction of an extension north from Golders Green to Edgware. Southern extensions to both the C&SLR and the Hampstead Tube soon followed.

Urbanization mushroomed in the wake of the extension to Edgware, which was a small village in a semi-rural area when the new tube terminus was first opened. By the end of the decade, the population had quadrupled and Edgware had become a commuter suburb.

The Metropolitan Railway remained independent of the Underground Group throughout the 1920s, but initiated a more deliberate urbanization process with the establishment of Metropolitan Railway Country Estates Limited in 1919. The task of this associate company was to exploit the post-war housing boom by developing housing estates on Metropolitan-owned land adjacent to the railway. This area to the north-west of London, including Wembley Park, Harrow, Northwood, Pinner and Rickmansworth was christened "Metro-land", and was soon attracting middle-class families from inner London. The Metropolitan ran an active publicity campaign, painting an idyllic picture of country life through its *Country Walks* booklets and Metro-land guides. Commuting was made easier by the extension of main-line electrification north of Harrow to Rickmansworth in 1925.

The 1920s were a productive period for architects. The Underground Group's staff architect, Stanley Heaps, designed the stations on the Golders Green to Edgware extension to blend in with the surrounding commuter developments. He placed neo-Georgian booking halls behind classical Doric columns of stone. Edgware station was his most flamboyant creation.

Frank Pick, then Joint Assistant Managing Director of the Underground, engaged the architect Charles Holden to design the seven new stations on the southern extension of the C&SLR from Clapham Common to Morden. At surface level the stations were built to a uniform design in Portland stone. The concept of a standard design, adaptable for each individual site, was carried through all Holden's stations to some extent, and was hugely influential in creating the distinctive

A surveyor checks his theodolite during
construction work at Tooting
Broadway station on the Morden
extension of the City and South
London Railway. The escalator shaft
and the curved foundation wall of
the booking hall are already taking
shape. The station opened on
13 September 1926.

Topical Press
March 1926

"house style" sought by Pick. Holden's involvement with the Underground was to continue throughout the 1920s and 1930s.

The 1920s were also a time of achievement for the buses as technical developments came thick and fast. At the beginning of the decade passengers suffered the indignities of travelling in solid-tyred boneshakers, open to all weathers. By the end of the 1920s they were riding in relative luxury in more spacious buses with smoother pneumatic tyres, covered tops and upholstered seats. The London General Omnibus Company introduced no fewer than five new bus designs between 1919 and 1930.

After the First World War, the social climate of Britain changed, and a new mobility was discovered with the expansion of transport services. The motor bus played a considerable part in this, particularly after 1921 when the LGOC started to operate services in association with other bus companies in an area designated "London Country". These services soon became popular. The working week became shorter, and people were encouraged to spend their increased leisure time enjoying trips to the countryside as far afield as Hitchin to the north and Horsham to the south of London. In July 1930 the LGOC set up its own coach subsidiary, known as Green Line Coaches Ltd, which provided a wide network of services within the Home Counties. Tram services remained stable during these years, but the shadow of the trolleybus was already on the horizon. Experiments with the design of trolleybuses, and proposals to use them to replace the trams, continued throughout the decade.

One event which seriously affected London's transport services during the 1920s was the nation-wide General Strike in support of coal miners. This lasted from 4 May to 14 May 1926. In all, 39,000 men from the Underground Group went out on strike, supported by 80 per cent of the Metropolitan Railway staff. Buses and trams were the worst hit as it was easier for strikers to obstruct the roads than the Underground system. The strike did not bring transport services to a complete standstill, however, as volunteers were enrolled to maintain services. Lord Ashfield, the Chairman of the Group, sent a calm but clear message to staff, indicating that he understood their sympathy towards the miners, but suggesting that they owed a higher loyalty and duty to the travelling public. The jobs of those who fulfilled that duty would be assured.

On the whole, the 1920s were a time of renewed vitality as the transport companies activated programmes which had lain dormant during the First World War. The extensive reconstruction and expansion of the Underground lines is well represented in the photographs from this period, while the street scenes indicate advances being made in bus design in terms of both comfort and safety. The 1920s ended on a positive and optimistic note for London Transport, and many of its projects were carried forward into the 1930s.

RIGHT: Tunnelling with pneumatic shovels during reconstruction work at the Mornington Crescent side of Camden Town Junction.

Topical Press
20 September 1922

BELOW: Tunnelling at Camden Town Junction within the Greathead Shield. James Henry Greathead was the engineer responsible for the construction of the very first deep tube, the City and South London Railway, which opened in 1890. He designed the tunnelling shield which takes his name. The tunnel was excavated by hand in front of the advancing shield, which provided a safe working environment and a temporary support for the clay, until cast-iron supporting sections were put in place. The same basic tunnelling principles have been used ever since to construct tube railways. The men in the chamber are using pneumatic drills to break through the earth, while men at the rear clear the debris.

Topical Press
October 1923

This photograph was taken during the construction of the southern extension of the City and South London Railway to Morden. Surveyors are working at street level on the Trinity Road station site (now Tooting Bec station).

Topical Press
February 1926

Construction of the escalators at
Clapham South station during the
southern extension of the City and
South London Railway.

Topical Press
2 March 1926

This photograph shows Jacob Epstein's sculpture "Night" as it was being created on the exterior of 55 Broadway. Epstein carved from the stone in situ. The intention was to make the sculpture an integral part of the building, rather than something imposed upon it. Tired of comments from nearby construction workers, Epstein had a shed built around the sculpture to gain some privacy.

Topical Press
8 May 1929

The headquarters of the Underground Group at 55 Broadway, built between 1927 and 1929 above St James's Park station, were designed by Charles Holden. The new office building replaced the old Electric Railway House from which the London General Omnibus Company, the Underground and the associated tram companies were all managed.

The fourteen-storey building, which occupies an awkward, irregular site, is decorated with Jacob Epstein's stone figures "Night" and "Day", and eight reliefs depicting the four winds by Henry Moore, Eric Gill, Allan Wyon, Eric Aumonier, A.M. Gerrard and F. Rabinovitch.

Topical Press
1931

Epstein standing beside his sculpture "Night". There was considerable public outcry when "Night" and "Day" were unveiled, as they were considered grotesque, even lewd. The Underground Group forced the sculptor to make last-minute changes to the sculpture "Day" in order to appease the most outraged members of the Board. The sculptures are still there today and no longer attract controversy.

Topical Press
8 May 1929

Charing Cross Hotel, built above the
station, dominates this photograph.
The Eleanor Cross in front of the
hotel is a copy, designed by E.M.
Barry in 1863, of the original cross
erected in 1290. When his wife,
Queen Eleanor of Castile, died,
Edward I had her body brought to
London from Nottinghamshire and
ordered 12 crosses to be erected
at the places where her funeral
cortège rested on its way to
Westminster Abbey. The last cross
was placed near the present site of
Trafalgar Square, then called
Charing. The replica cross was paid
for by the London, Chatham and
Dover Railway Company.

Topical Press
4 July 1923

LEFT: Waterloo Place, looking towards Lower Regent Street. Part of the equestrian statue of King Edward VII is just visible on the left, and the Crimea Memorial to the foot guards is on the far right of the photograph.

Topical Press
September 1923

BELOW: A London General Omnibus Company official gives advice to passengers at a bus queue in Trafalgar Square under the steady gaze of one of Sir Edwin Landseer's lions. This photograph was originally taken to illustrate the early type of LGOC ("General") bus stop. The LGOC adopted the fleet name "General" in 1906.

Topical Press
1921

A rainy day at Piccadilly Circus, looking
across to Regent Street. The old
Swan and Edgar store is on the left,
and the County Fire Office on the
right of the photograph.

Topical Press
July 1924

During the General Strike of 1926 barbed wire is attached to the bonnet of a bus under the watchful eye of a soldier armed with rifle and bayonet. This was done to prevent sabotage by strikers. The man at the wheel is probably a strikebreaker since he is not wearing a uniform.

Topical Press
May 1926

RIGHT: Tram track reconstruction taking place on Whitechapel High Street at Gardiners Corner. This work was part of the huge track reconstruction programme undertaken by the London County Council in 1929 in order to relieve chronic traffic congestion in the Whitechapel area.

Topical Press
April 1929

A policeman controls the traffic in front of South Africa House in Trafalgar Square. The bus on the right, with a covered top deck, is an NS-Type. The one on the left, with an open top, is an S-Type. After several experiments and failed applications for a licence, the London General Omnibus Company finally received permission from the Ministry of Transport to operate buses with covered tops in 1926.

Topical Press
6 June 1929

A fog flare mounted on a pavement stand illuminates the way for an electric tramcar during a particularly heavy bout of London smog. Before the Clean Air Act of 1956, which prohibited the emission of any smoke from chimneys, London was regularly shrouded in winter smog. The most memorable London smog occurred in December 1952 when more than 4,000 people died over a period of five days, mostly from related chest ailments.

Topical Press
1920–1930

LEFT: London General Omnibus
Company charabancs on a day trip
to Wendover in the Chilterns.
These were the early days of
motor coaches, before the
widespread private ownership
of cars.

Topical Press
May 1924

BELOW: A punting party lunch beside
the tow path at Hampton Court
at Whitsuntide.

Topical Press
1920–1930

A packed crowd for Derby Day. The
London General Omnibus
Company had its own private
enclosure at Epsom, and the tops
of the B-Type buses provided a
good view of the course, as well as
congenial picnic spots.

Newspaper Illustrated
c. 1920

LEFT: This photograph of Tooting Broadway station was taken just a year after it opened. Tooting Broadway was part of the southern extension of the City and South London Railway to Morden, and was one of Charles Holden's earliest station designs for the Underground.

Topical Press
29 April 1927

BELOW: A subway entrance to the newly reconstructed Piccadilly Circus station in front of the old Swan and Edgar store between Piccadilly and Regent Street.

Topical Press
May 1929

LEFT: Situated between Haymarket and Lower Regent Street, this is one of the three entrances to the original booking hall of Piccadilly Circus station. With its distinctive tiled surface and both the arched and round windows, it is a good example of the type of station designed by Leslie W. Green in the early 1900s. When Charles Holden re-designed the station in 1928, a new booking hall was constructed underneath the statue of Eros.

1925

BELOW: The forecourt at Edgware station. The station was designed by Stanley Heaps, the Underground company's chief architect, to blend in with the prevailing architecture of the developing commuter areas to the north of London.

Topical Press
3 July 1926

ABOVE: A passenger operates a ticket machine at Mansion House station. New types of automatic ticket machine were continually being developed. This one was relatively sophisticated for the time because it gave out change.

Topical Press
March 1928

RIGHT: Waiting for a lift at Goodge Street station on the Hampstead Tube.

Topical Press
12 May 1927

LEFT: An exhibition in the booking hall at Piccadilly Circus station, demonstrating the process of refrigeration by the Frigidaire Company. The large concourses of some Underground stations were occasionally used for exhibitions, displays and promotions.

Topical Press
2 August 1929

BELOW: The view from the bottom of a hydraulic lift shaft at Stockwell rail depot. This lift could hold a 15-ton railway carriage. It was used to transfer all City and South London Railway stock between the surface depot and the tunnels.

Topical Press
1922

ABOVE: Advertising murals painted by
Mary Adshead on the escalator
landing at Bank station.

Topical Press
January 1926

RIGHT: The finishing touches are added to
the murals above the escalator at
Piccadilly Circus station. There
were five panels, painted by the
artist Steven Bone, and depicting
various pursuits to be reached by
Underground, including work,
shopping and excursions to the
theatre and the countryside.
Passengers' attention was also
drawn to more distant horizons by
the central mural which showed
a pictorial map of the world,
with Piccadilly at the heart of
the British Empire.

Topical Press
17 March 1929

LEFT: Passengers waiting for a train at
Notting Hill Gate station when it
was part of the Metropolitan Line.

1919

LEFT: Passengers boarding a train at
Piccadilly Circus station.

Topical Press
6 December 1922

ABOVE: A driver using his portable
telephone set. By hooking the
terminals to the bare wires running
along the tunnel walls, a driver
could communicate quickly with the
substation attendant in the case of
an emergency.

Topical Press
11 August 1926

These photographs were taken for the London Electric Railway Company during the national railway strike of 1919. The strike, over wages and conditions, lasted from 26 September until 5 October, and was settled in the railwaymen's favour. In an effort to keep services running, the Underground took on thousands of volunteers to man the railway and provided facilities for the strikebreakers. Here, some volunteers catch up on sleep in passenger coaches from the Piccadilly Railway; others enjoy a morning dip in converted inspection pits.

G. Reeks
1919

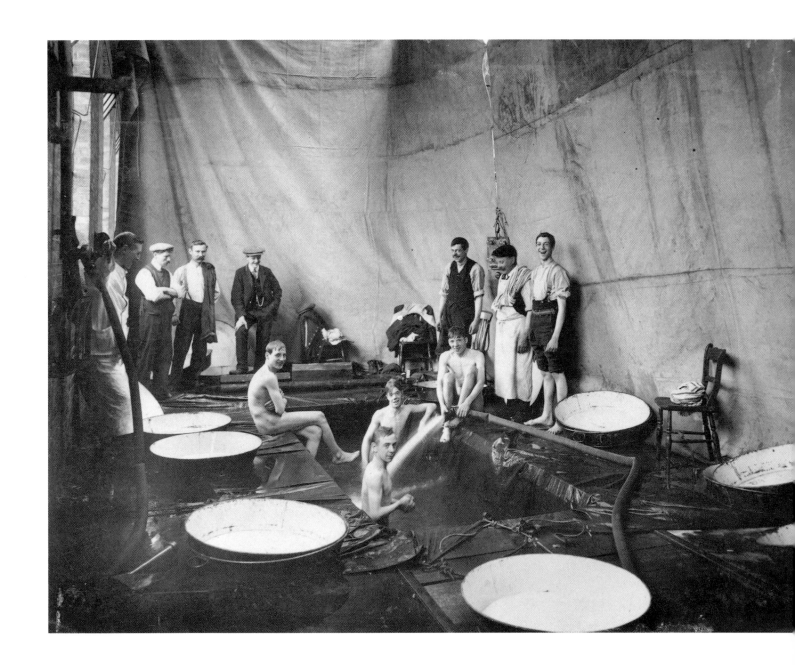

The signal cabin at Camden Town, showing a signalman, Alf Powell, operating the all-electric lever frame with his eye on the illuminated track indicator above. Camden Town has the busiest signal cabin on the Underground, controlling a complicated system of tunnels at the junction.

Topical Press
21 May 1924

Staff canteens were among the essential services which the Underground Group provided for its work-force. The size of this one at Acton Works reflects the large scale of the catering operation throughout its many depots, engineering works and garages and at strategically located Underground stations such as Hammersmith, Camden Town and Kennington. Menus were changed daily, and cooking facilities were also available for staff bringing their own food. The companies provided a large dining room at South Kensington for administrative staff, with another room above for dancing and other social activities.

Topical Press
November 1922

A New Image in the Thirties

The 1930s were years of intense activity and growth for London's transport systems. The London Passenger Transport Board, soon abbreviated to London Transport, was created on 1 July 1933 to bring London's buses, trams, trolleybuses and underground trains under one authority for the first time in the capital's history. Lord Ashfield was appointed Chairman of the Board, with Frank Pick as his deputy, and the two men quickly set about changing the face of London's transport in terms of both service and style.

One of the Board's first decisions was to replace petrol engines with diesel in all of its buses in order to reduce costs. This set a precedent for the whole country. By the end of the decade, London Transport had replaced more than half the bus fleet it had inherited in 1933 with new vehicles. In a further cost-cutting exercise, trolleybuses began to take over from trams, though the Second World War brought this venture to a temporary halt.

A huge modernization and extension scheme was initiated for the Underground, known as the 1935–40 New Works Programme, with the Government acting as loan guarantor. The scheme included rail extensions in north and east London, involving the Bakerloo, Northern and Central Lines. Some of the original steam-operated suburban branches of the London and North Eastern Railway were electrified under the Programme and linked to the tube network. With the opening of Cockfosters station on 31 July 1933, the northern extension of the Piccadilly Line from Finsbury Park was completed. The Piccadilly Line also ran the most modern rolling stock on the system in the early 1930s.

As well as improving travel through a more efficient and extensive service, Frank Pick wished to provide an agreeable environment for passengers. He also wanted to create a corporate design identity which would be recognizable to the travelling public throughout London, whatever the form of transport. He did this by introducing a design house style which incorporated everything from architecture, station furniture, vehicles and logos, to publicity. During his time with the Underground Group, Pick had already shown that a sense of unity could be achieved through design, and he worked on the same principle at London Transport.

The photographs in this chapter illustrate some of the achievements which took place in these crucial years. They show the extent of the construction work, which included Underground stations, complete with escalators and booking halls; miles of tunnel, track and bridges; bus, tram and trolleybus termini; as well as overhead wiring for the new trolleybuses. Some of the photographs take us behind the scenes to areas not immediately associated with passenger transport, such as the generating stations which powered the trains and trams. Frank Pick's house style is evident in the photographs of the stations designed by Charles Holden whose hallmark was an exquisite attention to detail, right down to the lighting in the booking halls and on the escalators. Many of the projects begun in the 1930s had to be curtailed with the onset of the Second World War. By the late 1940s Frank Pick was dead and Lord Ashfield was no longer Chairman, but their legacy to London Transport lived on for many years.

A sign is polished in readiness for the opening of Cockfosters station.

News Photos
August 1933

LEFT: Laying cables on the outer wall of a railway viaduct near Chiswick Park station. A temporary supporting structure has been built to allow work to proceed safely.

Topical Press
11 September 1931

BELOW: Reconstruction work following a Charles Holden design at Warren Street station.

Topical Press
7 October 1933

LEFT: Queensbury station was built as part of the Metropolitan branch from Wembley Park to Stanmore. Today it is part of the Jubilee Line.

Topical Press
29 June 1934

BELOW: Two workmen at the bottom of a shaft manoeuvre a skip of debris excavated from a tunnel during construction of the Piccadilly Line extension north from Finsbury Park.

Fox Photos
17 November 1930

PAGE 80: Southgate station at night.

Topical Press
26 May 1933

PAGE 81: The booking hall at Arnos
Grove station, built as part of
Charles Holden's grand design for
the Piccadilly Line extension to
Southgate. Free-standing wooden
ticket offices were abandoned on
the new extension in favour of
metal-framed ones with simulated
marble covering the bottom half.

Fox Photos
September 1932

LEFT: When redesigning Boston Manor
station, Holden added a tower with
panels of translucent glass up one
side which was illuminated at night.

Dell and Wainwright
24 December 1935

TOP RIGHT: St John's Wood Bakerloo
station (now on the Jubilee Line)
was designed by the staff architect,
Stanley Heaps, under the influence
of Charles Holden. Since this
photograph was taken, a month
after the station opened, a block of
flats has been built which detracts
somewhat from the symmetry of
the original design.

Topical Press
December 1939

RIGHT: The booking hall at Cockfosters
station, designed according to the
new London Transport house style
developed by Charles Holden.

Topical Press
September 1934

LEFT: The booking hall at Sudbury Town station, built in 1931. This was the prototype of Charles Holden's distinctive "box" shape design, which, together with his circular or "drum" shape, was to become a familiar sight on the Underground in the 1930s.

The standing lamps give light indirectly: light from a concealed source in the top of each stand is reflected off the white shapes in the bowls.

Fox Photos
1932

BELOW: Recently completed escalators and hall at Southgate station a month before it opened. Bronze uplighters, mounted between the escalators, reflect light off the ceiling. The magnificent standing lamps at the foot of the escalator shaft provided indirect illumination.

Topical Press
24 February 1933

Children boarding a District Line train at Ravenscourt Park for a day's outing to Eastcote near Harrow.

Topical Press
July 1934

The interior of a carriage on the
Piccadilly Line.

October 1935

A head-on view of one of the
experimental streamlined trains
used on the Piccadilly Line. The
most significant feature of these
new trains was the relocation of
the motor-driving equipment under
the floor, which created extra
passenger space. Streamlining was
abandoned in the final design which
became known as 1938 tube stock.

Topical Press
November 1936

Father Christmas goes Underground.
    After an exhibition of British-made
    toys held at Charing Cross station
    booking hall, London Transport
    distributed the toys to children's
    hospitals.

Topical Press
24 December 1931

The old staff canteen at Hounslow
    Garage just before it was rebuilt in
    1937. The driver and conductor on
    the right have also stopped to refill
    their billycans, which can be seen
    on the shelf behind them. The sign
    above the servery prohibiting
    gambling suggests that the bus
    company kept strict codes of
    conduct for its staff. The swastika,
    originally a primitive religious
    symbol, was often used for
    decorative purposes, but was
    acquiring sinister associations at
    the time.

Topical Press
1937

Trainee conductors receiving instruction
on a bus at the Central Buses
Training School at Chiswick bus
works. The School provided
extensive training for busmen, with
plenty of facilities for practical
experience of driving buses and
collecting fares.

Topical Press
April 1935

LEFT: A ticket clerk waits for customers in one of the new-style booking offices at Chiswick Park station. The ticket offices are known as passimeters after an American invention devised to count or "meter" passengers electrically as they pass through a turnstile under a ticket window. They were originally free-standing ticket booths which issued tickets automatically, doing away with the need for ticket inspectors on inward journeys. The first passimeter was installed on 16 December 1921 at Kilburn Park on the Bakerloo Line.

Topical Press
3 August 1933

RIGHT: Using an information machine at Leicester Square station. Throughout its history, London Transport has tried various ways of providing quick and easily understood directions through its complex network. The most successful still in use today is the diagrammatic Underground map designed by Harry Beck in 1931.

Topical Press
September 1937

RIGHT: The Prince of Wales (later Edward VIII) during a visit to Wood Green substation. Accompanied by UERL Chairman Lord Ashfield, the Prince spent a day inspecting the British-made electrical equipment on the new Piccadilly Line western and northern extensions. He travelled on the tube between Wood Green and Hyde Park Corner where he met staff who had worked on the City and South London Railway, opened by his father in 1890.

Topical Press
14 February 1933

Ludgate Circus was constructed between
1864 and 1875 at the junction of
Ludgate Hill and Fleet Street.
The railway viaduct was built by the
London Chatham and Dover
Railway in 1865 to reach Ludgate
Hill station. A year later the line
was extended to link with the
Metropolitan Railway at Farringdon.
The viaduct, a familiar feature of
the City of London, was pulled
down as recently as 1990.

Topical Press
11 April 1930

A combined bus and tram stop in front
of the Marlborough Cinema,
Holloway Road. The film "Lightning
Conductor", which starred Gordon
Harker as a London Transport bus
conductor, was showing when this
photograph was taken.

Topical Press
June 1939

A trolleybus turning in front of the London Central Meat Market at Smithfield, Clerkenwell. Originally a field outside the City walls, it was known as far back as the Middle Ages as a horse and cattle market. Bartholomew Fair was held there from 1123 until 1855, when it was closed because of the debauched behaviour of its patrons. Smithfield also has a gruesome history as a place of public execution for criminals, witches, heretics and religious martyrs.

The London Central Meat Market opened at Smithfield in 1868. Six years after this photograph was taken, this corner of the market and the trolleybus lines were devastated by a German flying bomb.

Topical Press
June 1938

ABOVE: Hailing the number 11 bus at a request stop on the Strand. This photograph was originally taken to illustrate a type of bus stop. Even though it looks somewhat posed, it is a good example of the care that was taken to create a well-proportioned and interesting composition and to place the subject in context.

Topical Press
14 July 1937

RIGHT: One of the subway entrances to Bank station, photographed from the Royal Exchange. The building directly opposite is the Mansion House, the official residence of the Lord Mayor of London since 1752. The equestrian statue is that of the Duke of Wellington, cast in bronze from captured French guns in recognition of the Duke's support of the bill for the rebuilding of London Bridge between 1823 and 1831.

Topical Press
1936

People taking advantage of the summer
weather to motor out into the
countryside. This photograph was
taken at Box Hill, near Reigate
in Surrey, and indicates the
extensive area covered by
London's bus companies. Before
the Second World War, the bus
was the cheapest and easiest
way for Londoners to get to
the countryside.

Daily Mail
1931

Two views of the Shaftesbury Memorial Fountain and Eros in the foundry of A.B. Burton at Thames Ditton, Surrey. The statue had been taken there for repairs following serious damage to the memorial during New Year's Eve festivities in 1931. The statue was cast in aluminium and the fountain was bronze. The golden colour of the basin and the greenish-bronze of the pedestal, topped with a silvery Eros must have created a startlingly colourful sight at the memorial's unveiling.

January 1932

Better known as Eros for the winged figure in mid-flight on the top, the Shaftesbury Memorial was originally executed by the sculptor Alfred Gilbert as a memorial fountain in commemoration of the philanthropist Lord Shaftesbury. It was unveiled on 29 June 1893. The fountain has been moved and altered several times, but was recently restored to its former glory and re-erected close to its original site in Piccadilly Circus.

Topical Press
August 1933

LEFT: Lots Road power station at Chelsea, photographed from the south side of the Thames. Opened in 1905, it was built to serve the Underground Group companies, including parts of the tram network. It is still the main source of power for the Underground, although electricity is also taken from the national grid.

O. Hoppe
c. 1935

RIGHT: The construction of a turbine at Lots Road power station during a modernization programme in the early 1930s. The aim was to increase the output capacity of the generating station and replace old machinery.

Topical Press
1 April 1931

RIGHT: A view of Lots Road power station turbine hall from the control room.

Topical Press
26 June 1934

LEFT: Linesmen repairing trolleybus
overhead wires at Fulwell Depot.
This kind of maintenance work was
done at night to cause the minimum
disruption to services.

Dell and Wainwright
29 January 1936

ABOVE: A workman at the top of a tower
platform changing light fittings on
the mast high above Enfield West
(now Oakwood) station.

Topical Press
28 June 1934

LEFT: A permanent way gang replacing
rails at Marble Arch station. Many
of these men would soon be asked
to serve in the coming war, hinted
at in the poster on the left which
calls for the defence of Britain.

Topical Press
May 1938

ABOVE: Posters are changed on the
Underground during the night while
the electric current is off and the
trains are not running.

Topical Press
11 February 1931

A City at War

The announcement on 3 September 1939 that Britain was at war had been expected, and London Transport had already made contingency plans. An Air Raid Precautions (ARP) Committee had been meeting since 1937, and London Transport staff were receiving regular training in first aid, rescue operations and fire-fighting, before the war started.

The modernization and reconstruction work of the 1935-40 New Works Programme had to stop. The major task of London Transport now was to keep the city's transport services running safely, even in the event of an air attack. Floodgates and watertight doors were installed in anticipation of a bomb penetrating a tunnel under the Thames and flooding the central Underground system. Netting was applied to the windows of all vehicles, including Underground trains, to reduce the risk of splintering glass during a bomb blast. All transport services were reduced; bus services were heavily curtailed to save fuel and to minimize the risks of operating during the blackout; Underground, tram and trolleybus operations were also cut, but a service of some kind was nearly always maintained, even through the worst of the Blitz which began in September 1940.

Even though its services were reduced, London Transport was kept busy supporting the war effort. One of its biggest tasks at the start of the war was to take a major part in the mass evacuation of London's children, pregnant women and hospital patients to the country. In 1940 it formed its own Home Guard unit which grew to 30,000 members. The Underground played host to a varied clientele. Disused station platforms were converted into emergency headquarters for the London Transport Board and the National Railway Executive Committee. The Government had appointed the latter to oversee London Transport and the main-line railways. The Anti-Aircraft Command took over Brompton Road station as its operations centre, and the Office of Works used part of a tunnel at Aldwych to store national treasures from the British Museum.

London Transport's most famous guests were the shelterers. As the Blitz got under way, Londoners realized that the safest place to be was underground and people literally moved in. It soon became clear that arrangements for shelterers would have to be formalized and organized on a large scale with proper sanitation, first-aid posts, bunk-style sleeping accommodation, refreshment provisions and even entertainment. Sadly, the tube shelters were not totally immune from bombing and there were fatalities during six separate incidents in which Underground stations were hit.

As well as providing transport and shelter, London Transport made a special contribution to the war effort by turning its newly-built rail depot at Aldenham into an aircraft factory to produce over 700 Halifax bombers. It joined forces with four motor companies to form the London Aircraft Production Group which built the planes. London Transport staff themselves raised enough money to pay for two Spitfires, at £5,000 each. Both bore the London Passenger Transport Board's bulls-eye symbol. Other workshops supported the war effort by manufacturing shells, landing craft, parts for tanks and much more, as well as carrying out their

Two London Transport employees, Mrs I. Vance (on the left) and Mrs E. Clements, act as "spotters", looking out for enemy aircraft from the roof of London Transport's Griffith House offices. Staff there were very active on the Air Raid Precautions Committee, serving as fire-watchers, fire-fighters, spotters and shelter wardens.

Topical Press
19 May 1941

normal tasks. Aircraft components were manufactured by the Plessey Company in the newly completed Central Line tunnels between Leytonstone and Gants Hill.

Women were responsible for much of this war work. In all, 16,500 additional female staff were employed by London Transport to replace male staff called up for service in the armed forces. Although women had been recruited by the transport companies during the First World War, their role had been limited to certain tasks; during the Second War, they did virtually all the jobs vacated by the men, apart from driving. Women seized the opportunity enthusiastically and many became highly skilled. They worked in bus garages, railway depots, engineering works and overhaul depots, as well as staffing the stations, serving as conductors and running canteens. They were also employed at power stations and in factories producing armaments – half the staff working on the Halifax bombers were women.

The photographs in this chapter are imbued with the atmosphere of a city at war. The horror of the air raids is palpable in the photographs of adults and children huddled together in the uncertain safety of the Underground shelters, their lives disjointed and their families uprooted from their homes. The dreadful reality of those raids is realized even more in photographs of the enormous and crippling damage caused by the bombs which rained down, night after night, during the Blitz.

However, the photographs also portray the camaraderie which developed among the London Transport staff as they went about their war work under increasingly difficult conditions. Sheer enjoyment of their work is evident in the faces of the women as they take on tasks considered, before the war, to be "men's work". Even the seriousness of the activities of the ARP Committee and the Home Guard unit is tinged with light humour.

RIGHT: A carriage cleaner takes a break in the doorway of a train driver's cab.

Fox Photos
1941

BELOW: Canteen Assistant, Mrs Olive White, shares a joke with a colleague in the canteen at Nunhead Garage, South East London. Mrs White, the widow of a tram conductor, worked at Nunhead for four years through some of the worst air raids of the Blitz. Her own home was blasted three times but she was only absent from work once.

Topical Press
20 July 1944

RIGHT: Four conductors model their new uniforms for press photographers. The helmets were issued as a precaution but were not normally worn on duty.

Keystone Press
1940

BELOW: Mrs Marion Callow, a former waitress, working as a pipe-fitter's mate in the repair shop at Acton Railway Works.

Topical Press
28 June 1943

RIGHT: London Transport became heavily involved in manufacturing aircraft during the Second World War. It joined forces with four motor companies to form the London Aircraft Production Group which completed over 700 Handley Page Halifax bombers for the Ministry of Aircraft Production between 1941 and 1945.
The young woman in this photograph is putting the finishing touches to a Halifax bomber at Leavesden, near Watford, one of the workshops London Transport converted for aircraft production.

1941–1944

These women are operating a lathe at
Acton Railway Works.

Topical Press
23 May 1942

LEFT: Looking through a protected
window on a train. Netting was
glued to the windows of all London
Transport vehicles to reduce
splintering during bomb blasts.

Fox Photos
1940

LEFT: Fire-fighting was an important part
of the Air Raid Precaution training
which London Transport staff
received from the very beginning of
the war. It proved invaluable during
the Blitz of 1940–41. These two
fire-fighters belonged to a squad at
Chiswick Works, where a new fire
station was erected as a protective
measure before war was declared.

Topical Press
20 March 1941

ABOVE: During the Second World War
women were recruited in large
numbers to take over the
traditionally male jobs left vacant
when men were called up for
active service. In this photograph a
porter assists a passenger on the
platform. Women were first
employed as porters by the
Underground at Chancery Lane
station in September 1940.

Daily Mirror
1940

RIGHT: A soldier, home on leave, stands with his daughter in front of a mock gas chamber during an exhibition at Charing Cross Underground station illustrating protection against war gases.

Topical Press
14 August 1941

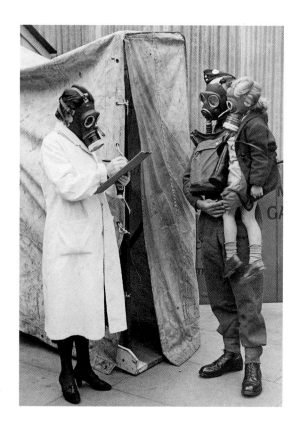

BELOW: Underground staff were encouraged to join in the knitting campaign of the War Comforts Fund Association (Warco). At one point 12,000 members of staff were knitting clothing for the troops serving overseas and for the 24 London Transport employees being held as prisoners of war in Germany.

Snook and Son
1940

Air-raid spotters beside a shelter on
Hungerford Bridge at Charing
Cross. The steel bell shelters were
erected at vulnerable sites on the
Underground, and were intended
to be used by one or two staff
members for short periods during
air raids.

Topical Press
24 April 1941

Air-raid damage to the tram track at
Westminster Bridge Road and
Kennington Road, opposite
Lambeth North station.

Topical Press
16 May 1941

Severe damage to the recently
modernized station buildings at
Sloane Square which received a
direct hit at 10.00 p.m., just as a
crowded train was leaving the
station. A lump of concrete went
right through one of the coaches
and the new escalators were
destroyed.

Topical Press
13 November 1940

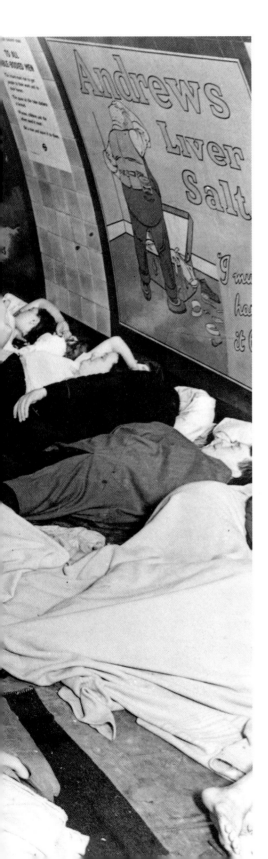

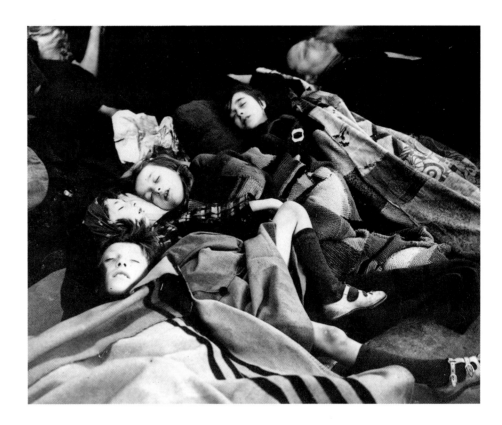

LEFT: Tube shelterers sleeping on the lower concourse of an Underground station. As the bombing increased, more and more Londoners began to seek shelter from the Blitz in the tube stations. Bunks were installed, and lavatories, medical-aid posts and refreshment services provided. At some stations there were even lending libraries and educational centres.

Topical Press
10 October 1940

ABOVE: Sleeping children sheltering from the Blitz at an Underground station.

Fox Photos
1940

19**45** *to* 19**50**

The Post-War Years

It was to be some time before London Transport could recover from the body blows it received during the Second World War, particularly given the political and economic climate of the time. The Labour Party came to power in 1945, bringing with it a plan to nationalize public utilities. At the beginning of 1948 the British Transport Commission was born and the old London Passenger Transport Board was replaced by a new London Transport Executive under the auspices of the Commission.

London Transport had to join the queue at the British Transport Commission, which had many pressing demands on its budgets in war-torn Britain. Money was no longer available for the New Works Programme, interrupted by the war, and London Transport was only allowed to complete the eastern and western extensions of the Central Line to Epping and West Ruislip respectively. The Epping to Ongar section was still operated by steam trains as late as 1957. The scheme to electrify the section of the Northern Line between Mill Hill East and Edgware, and the branch line to Alexandra Palace were also abandoned.

Instead of replacing trams with trolleybuses as planned before the war started, it was decided to bring in diesel buses. This was partly because the proposed use of the trams' electrical distribution network was no longer so financially attractive now that the tramway system was in a bad state of repair and needed replacing, and partly because diesel buses offered more flexibility than trolleybuses.

One major international attraction occurring in Britain during this early post-war period was the Olympic Games, held in the summer of 1948. London Transport put on extra train services to Wembley Stadium where the main events were held. Wembley Park station was enlarged to cope with the crowds attending the Olympics from all over Britain and overseas.

The London Transport Film Unit began operating under the auspices of the London Transport Publicity Department during this period. It commissioned films of London Transport's activities, the first being "Seven More Stations" about the opening of the Central Line extension. Many stills from the Unit's films became part of the Museum's photographic collection, and some appear in this book.

The small number of photographs that appear in this section reflects the low-key profile of London Transport as it struggled to come to terms with a period of post-war gloom, financial constraints and new masters. Not until the 1950s was London Transport to recapture some of its old vigour and vitality.

A team of construction workers about to be lowered underground during the building of new subways at Waterloo Underground station.

Colin Tait
1949

Ticket machines in operation at Piccadilly
Circus station.

Walter A. Curtin
October 1948

RIGHT: A film crew from the Academy Picture Corporation shooting "Seven More Stations", a film about the Central Line extensions, for the London Transport Film Unit. They are using a plate-layer's trolley instead of the traditional dolly. Directed by Victor Sheridan, "Seven More Stations" received its première at the Odeon Cinema, Leicester Square on 21 July 1948. This photograph was taken as a publicity shot for the film. The Film Unit was established after the war to commission films for London Transport's Publicity Office.

Photo Centre Ltd
19 July 1948

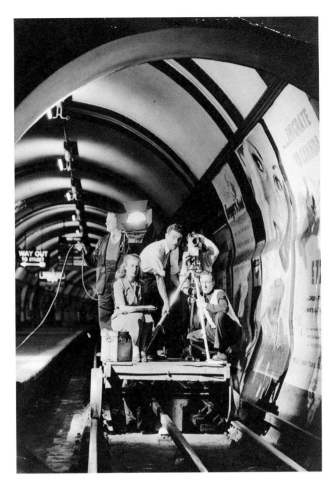

BELOW: This photograph of the subway at Tottenham Court Road station was taken specifically to illustrate one of the many strategic advertising sites reserved by Lilley & Skinner.

Topical Press
July 1946

LEFT: Trolleybus conductor, Mrs L.M. Thurgar, on duty ready to collect fares, and BELOW: playing dominoes with two colleagues in the canteen at Hammersmith Bus Depot.

Topical Press
30 July 1947

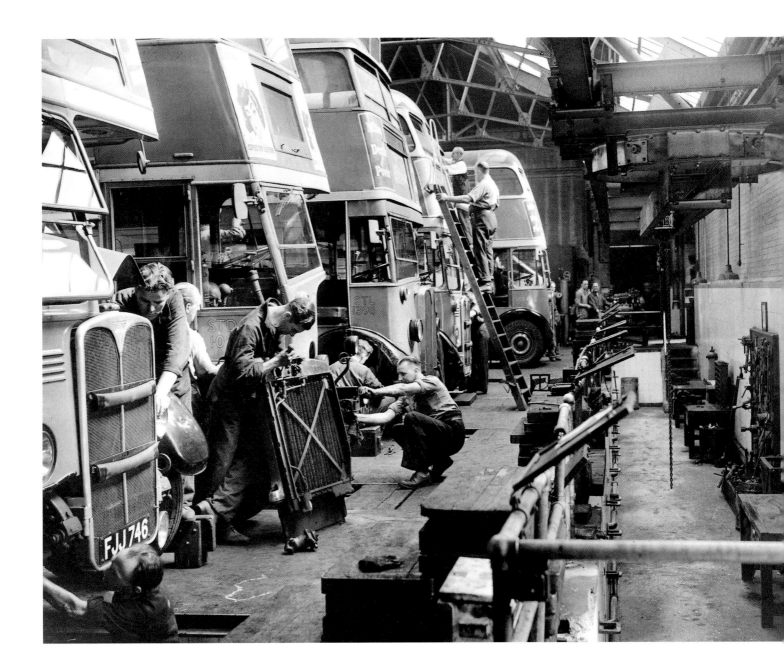

Maintenance men at work in the docking
bays at Victoria Bus Garage.

Colin Tait
August 1949

An interior view of a crowded
Metropolitan Line train.

Topical Press
1948

The last tram on route 31 leaves
Southampton Row for its final
journey to Wandsworth before
being scrapped. The trams were
gradually replaced by diesel buses.

Colin Tait
30 September 1950

1950 to 1965

Modernizing the System

In many ways the 1950s and 1960s were a time of renewal for London Transport after a period of post-war austerity. This was despite a reduction in the demand for services, with television keeping people at home and car ownership growing at a rapid, and alarming, rate in view of London's increasingly congested roads. Although the population of London itself declined after the war, the new towns blossomed beyond the recently determined Green Belt as people moved away from the city. The demand for the Green Line coaches and country bus services increased, and the area of their operations was expanded. New garages were built at some of the new towns in the late 1950s to service the needs of these expanding routes.

The population shifts away from London meant that London Transport had difficulties recruiting staff to run the buses on these extensive routes. Although the majority of women had relinquished their jobs when the men returned from the war, London Transport now resumed its war-time policy of recruiting female conductors on equal pay. Women were once again brought in to fill the breach and this time they stayed.

The tram replacement programme was completed and, after a protracted and emotional farewell, London said goodbye to its last tram at New Cross Depot on 6 July 1952. The trolleybuses were also to be replaced by diesel buses but outlived the trams by ten years.

The new bus which took over from the trolleybus was very special. London Transport announced the arrival of the Routemaster in 1954. This bus could carry more passengers than its predecessor, the RT, but it was light, being built largely of aluminium, the gears were fully automatic and it had power-assisted steering and independent suspension. The prototype RMI was fully tested for two years before entering service, along with three other prototypes. Full operation of the fleets of Routemaster buses began in 1959. Londoners quickly appreciated the comfort, efficiency and smooth running of their new bus, affectionately known as the "RM". It is still the favourite London bus today, not least because of the ease of getting on and off the open platform at the back and the additional service of a conductor.

Larger and better facilities were needed for the new bus fleets. Since the proposed plans for the Northern Line extension from Edgware had been abandoned, it was decided to convert the unfinished railway depot at Aldenham into a bus overhaul works. This was completed in 1956. Buses received a thorough overhaul and steam-clean every three or four years. A new bus garage construction programme began in the early 1950s. The designs for some of these garages were reminiscent of the days of Frank Pick, when form and function were both an integral part of any building plans. Architects incorporated the new post-war developments in building techniques and material into their designs, to create an innovative and refreshingly different approach to what were basically very utilitarian buildings.

The Underground also modernized much of its rolling stock in the late 1950s and 1960s. The bodywork of the new trains was of unpainted aluminium alloy and had become standard by 1956. The Metropolitan Line finally caught up with the other lines in the early 1960s, with the electrification of the routes from Rickmansworth to Amersham and Chesham.

The first important challenge of the 1950s for London Transport was the Festival of Britain in 1951 which brought thousands of people to the capital. In 1950 it sent four new buses on a European tour of seven countries to advertise the event and to attract overseas visitors. The announcement, carried in several languages on the buses, summed up the message behind the tour: "A nation-wide demonstration … of Britain's continuing contributions to civilisation and of her faith in her future place in the world". The improvements and renovations carried out at Charing Cross and Waterloo stations were timed for the opening of the Festival at the nearby South Bank where the main exhibitions were held. These stations were intended to be "worthy gateways to the South Bank Exhibition", according to Lord Latham, Chairman of London Transport at the time.

Other plans for the Festival included eight special bus services; increased rail services; links between the South Bank, the Festival Pleasure Gardens at Battersea and the coach and car parks; and the provision of a special enquiry office at Charing Cross station, and a Festival travel map. Over 100,000 visitors a day were expected to visit the Festival which was opened on 3 May by the King and ran until the end of September. Its main purpose was to portray British achievements, past and present, in the fields of art, science, architecture and industry. London Transport exhibited one of its new aluminium-bodied Underground trains at the Festival.

In the 1960s London Transport's most significant achievement was the construction of the Victoria Line which opened in stages between 1968 and 1971. Technical planning, feasibility studies and experimental tunnelling were all advanced by the early 1960s and the go-ahead was given in August 1962. The major construction work began in early 1963. The Victoria Line was the first new railway to be built under central London since the early 1900s and, when it opened, was the most advanced of its kind in the world. Its construction heralded an era of new Underground projects which came to fruition in the following decades.

The photographs featured in this final chapter indicate the new approach to commissioned photography on the part of the London Transport Publicity Department. After the war, as well as maintaining the programme of record photography, taken for many years by Topical Press, the Department commissioned independent photographers to take more artistic and individual photographs, in the hope of attracting a wider public to the collection through the pages of the London Transport staff magazine. The results can be seen in photographs of maintenance staff working "behind the scenes", and often at night, at jobs of which the travelling public are only vaguely aware. The new buses and trains, the bus garage construction programme, and the presence of more women staff on the buses and stations, all reflect the more upbeat atmosphere which followed the post-war gloom.

RIGHT and PAGE 141: Perhaps one of the least-known jobs performed by London Transport staff is that of the "fluffers" who clean the tunnels every night. No machine has yet been invented which can do the job of removing the fluff, dirt and human hair which accumulate in the tunnels each day. This back-breaking work is still done mainly by women.

Topical Press
January 1952

LEFT: In the early 1950s, rat catchers used ferrets to keep the Underground tunnels free of rats. These men are about to finish their shift, taking their night's haul of rats with them.

Colin Tait
January 1950

LEFT: Essential maintenance and cleaning
of the Underground system is
carried out during the night when
the trains have stopped running.
This man is cleaning the ventilator
shaft at Hyde Park Corner station.

Colin Tait
January 1950

ABOVE: Taking a break during routine
night cleaning of the ventilator
shafts under the booking hall at
Piccadilly Circus.

Topical Press
January 1952

In the early 1950s, London Transport instituted a new programme of bus garage construction. The most impressive of these was Stockwell Garage, designed by Adie, Button and Partners. At the time of its construction in 1951–52, it had the largest expanse of roof, without intermediate support, in Europe. This arched, reinforced-concrete roof allowed space for 200 buses.

J. Somerset Murray
October 1953

The very first Routemaster (RM) bus is given a "tilt" test at Aldenham Bus Works before going into service. This was the prototype, numbered RM1, which entered passenger service in February 1956. The production model RMs were introduced in November 1959, and came to epitomize the "red London bus".

Colin Tait
January 1956

LEFT: Every day thousands of people go
up and down these steps at
Piccadilly Circus which are kept in
good condition by routine night
maintenance.

Topical Press
January 1952

ABOVE: Heavy traffic in Regent Street as
the crowds make their annual
pilgrimage to the West End to see
the Christmas decorations.

Colin Tait
December 1957

1950 TO 1965

148 — 149

A passenger tenders her money for a
tube ticket.

Walter A. Curtin
January 1951

A crowded platform at Piccadilly Circus
station.

J. Somerset Murray
1952

This photograph was taken to illustrate
an experiment to increase window
space by modifying the roof of a
tube car.

Colin Tait
1950

RIGHT: The interior of a train, illustrating
experimental lean-to seats which
increased the standing capacity of a
tube car by 16 passengers.

Colin Tait
15 December 1953

Staff at the railway training school
adjoining Lambeth North station
adjust their hats.

Colin Tait
December 1950

Staff raise their cups to the departure of
the old trams during the tram
replacement scheme. New diesel
buses took over from trams after
the war.

Colin Tait
30 September 1950

An anxious mother and child at the
    counter of the Lost Property Office
    at Baker Street station.

Walter A. Curtin
1951

LEFT: The main exhibition site for the 1951 Festival of Britain on the South Bank, photographed from Victoria Embankment.

Colin Tait
April 1951

RIGHT: In 1950, four new London buses were sent on a tour of Europe to promote the forthcoming Festival of Britain. This photograph shows one of the buses being loaded on to a ship at the beginning of the tour.

Topical Press
28 July 1950

RIGHT: In an effort to generate optimism, pride and national enthusiasm after the gloom and austerity of the war years, the Government subsidized and promoted new works of art, mostly exhibited on the South Bank as part of the 1951 Festival of Britain. The Festival paid homage to contemporary British design, art, architecture and sculpture, and aided and encouraged young modernists, as well as the more established artists and sculptors. The sculpture in this photograph is *The Islanders* by Siegfried Charoux on the exterior of the Sea and Ships Pavilion at the South Bank.

Topical Press
18 May 1951

LEFT: Operating a points lever during shunting at Northfields Depot.

Colin Tait
March 1955

RIGHT: A conductor, Ms A. Hart, poses on the boarding platform of a bus.

H. Zinram
14 March 1962

Photograph numbers